Starting Macro Photography

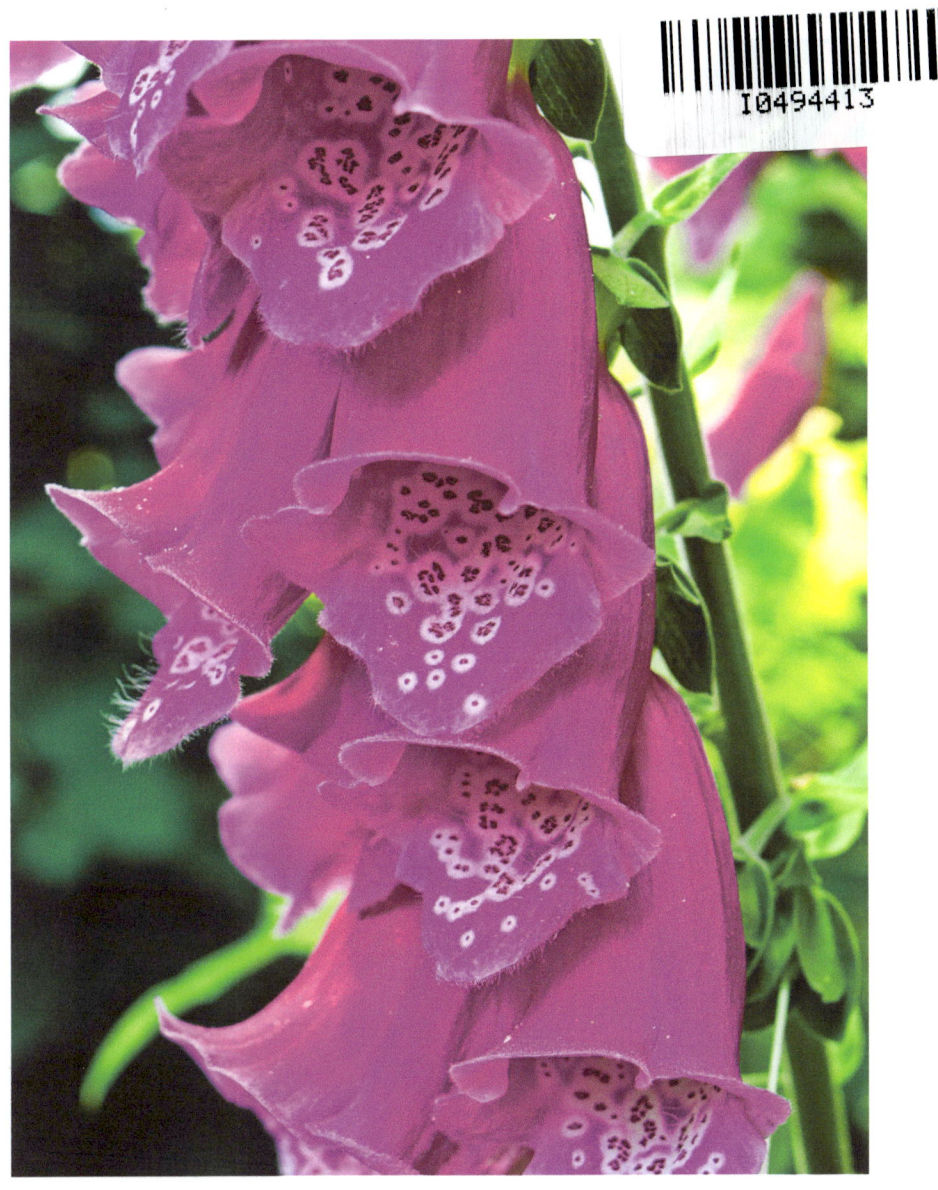

David Bigwood, LRPS

Published by davidbigwoodpublishing.wordpress.com

Copyright Notice

Table of Contents

About the Author

David Bigwood is a regularly published writer and photographer with his work having been used in well over sixty publications, mainly in Australia and the United Kingdom.

He is a Licentiate of the Royal Photographic Society and a member of the Australian Society of Authors.

For three years he was a columnist on freelancing for the UK magazine F2 Freelance and Digital. He has written regularly for *Australian Photography* and has also written for *Australian Camera* and *Better Photography*.

He founded and edited *The Black and White Enthusiast* magazine (later *Silvershotz*) and was sometime editor of the Journal of the Australian Photography Society.

He has images with Alamy, the on-line photography library.

Starting Macro Photography

When I moved to the Snowy Mountains in New South Wales, Australia I discovered the wildflowers that carpet the alpine meadows in the summer. My camera worked overtime but I lacked the ability to get really close to the blooms which was a disappointment as some of them were tiny but colourful and delicate and cried out for a really close up shot. I needed a macro lens but at that time cash was at a premium so I just put it on my wish list

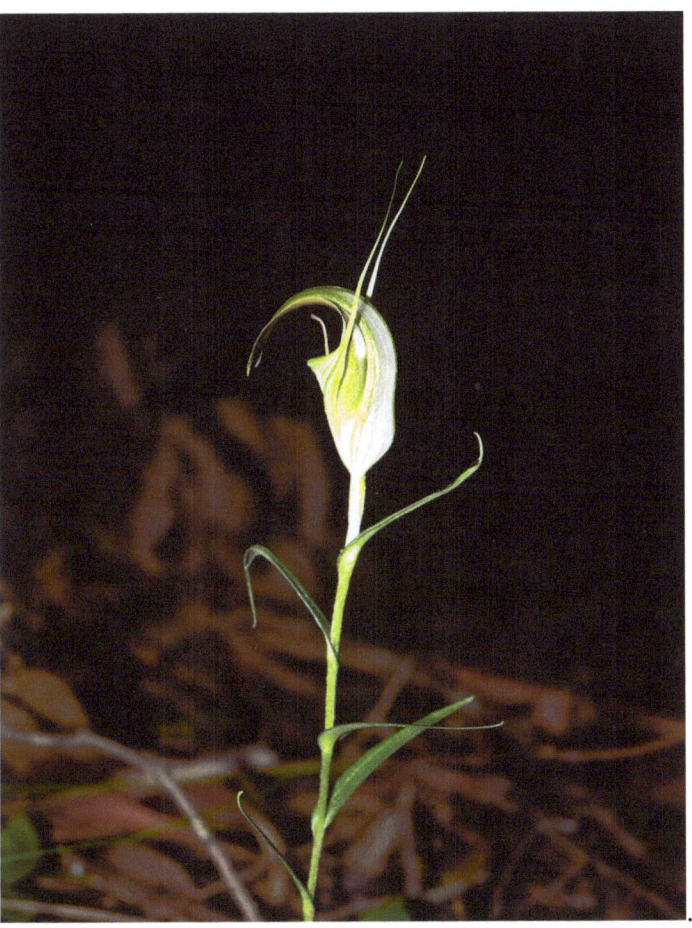

Greenhood orchid shot with standard lens. A macro lens or a 10 dioptre close up lens would have enabled me to get in close to this tiny plant.

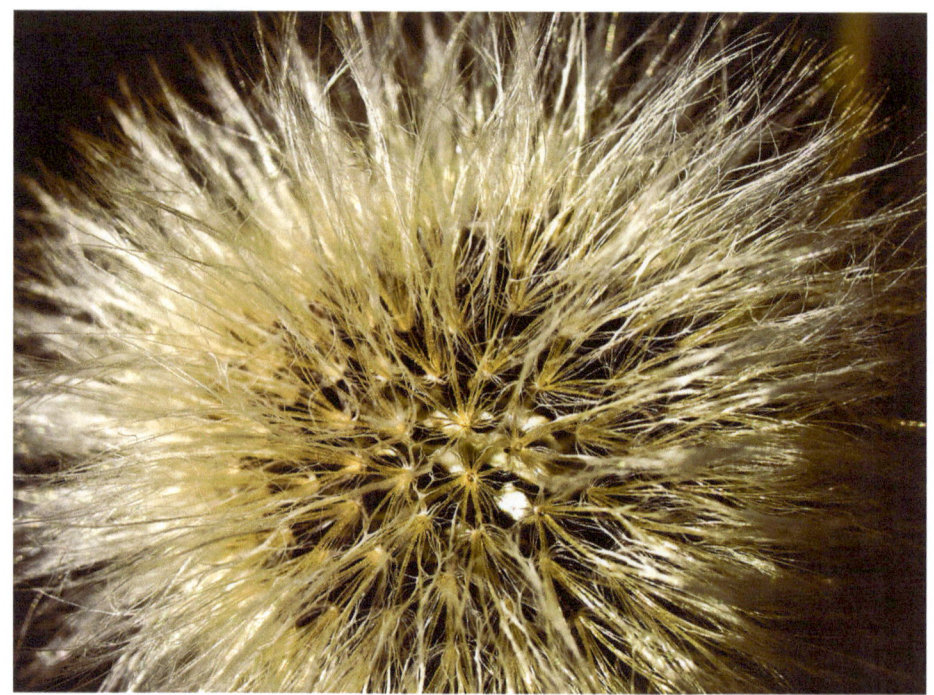

This seed head was just 2cms across but photographed with my macro lens, it fills the frame.

Then I came across a book, *The Digital Photographer's Guide to Filters* (David and Charles, 978-0-7153-2654-1) by Ross Hoddinott, a young nature photographer whom I had interviewed a few years previously. His close up images of nature subjects had always impressed me along with numerous editors so I was fascinated to read that he often uses close up lenses for these brilliant pictures. This surprised me as I had assumed that he would have been using macro lenses that are designed for very close work. In fact, in his book he championed the close up lens over the macro for a variety of reasons; lightness for one and cost.

It was the cost factor that really interested me at that stage so I investigated and found that close up lenses generally come in a set of three — 1, 2, and 4 dioptre — to screw into the filter thread on the front of a camera lens. Ross's endorsement encouraged me to buy a set that I found on the internet for $35. As a bonus a 10 dioptre lens was thrown in. This would give me the ability to test my close up work without spending too much. Admittedly, my purchase was a cheap one; the sort of close up lenses that Ross was using would probably have cost several times as much. However, I did get some acceptable results while using them and that did whet my appetite for close

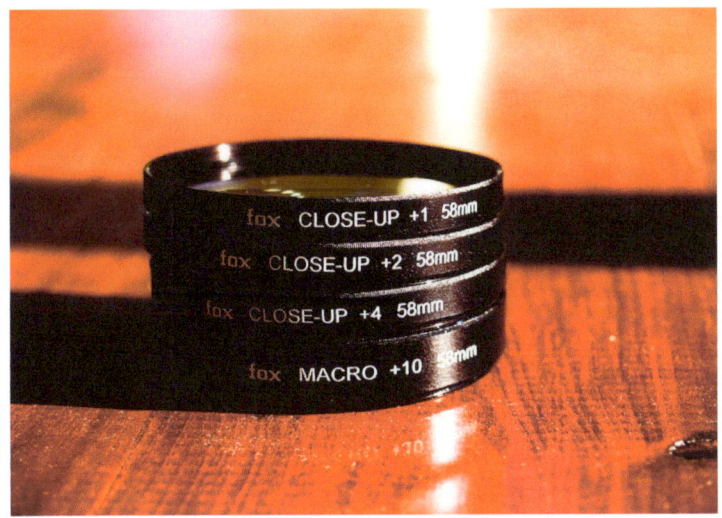

A set of close up lenses

up photography.

Of course, I had been shooting some close up images before getting these lenses as my DSLR was able to focus reasonably closely especially if I set the short zoom lens to its maximum focal length or used my longer zoom lens. Compact digital cameras can also get in close but you will not be able to blur the background to concentrate attention on the subject as you can with a DSLR and even a DSLR with a standard lens will not be able to blur the background as much as a macro lens can.

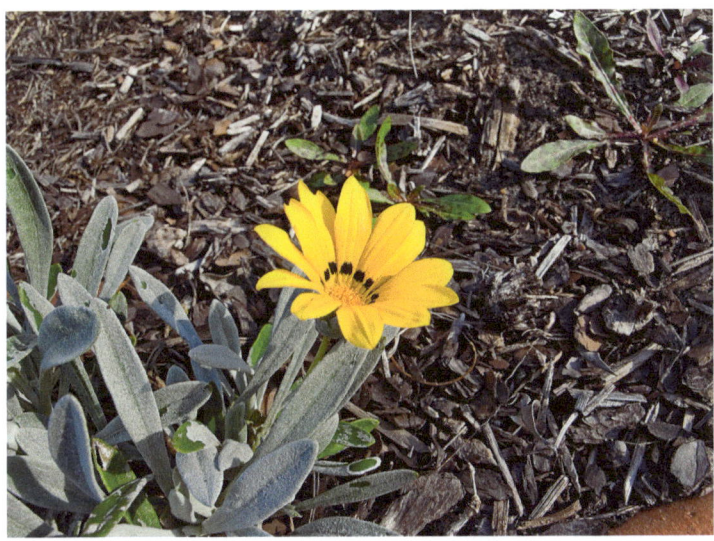

Shot without close up lens

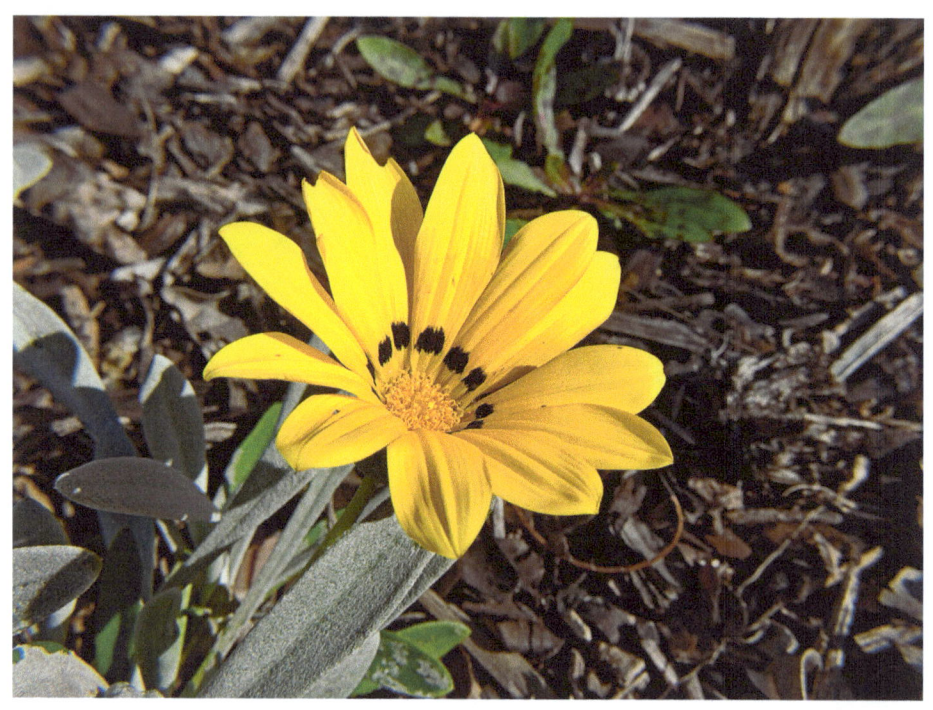

Shot with a 2 dioptre close up lens

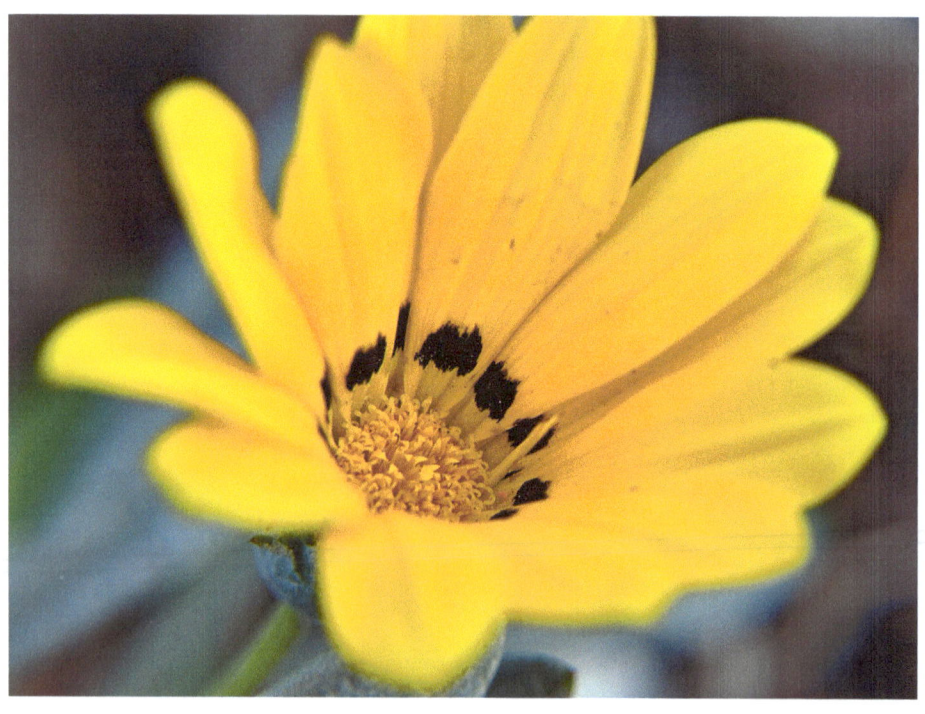

Shot with a 10 dioptre close up lens

Eventually, after some months of using the close up lenses, I decided that I liked getting in close to a subject and decided to splash out and buy a macro lens. I purchased a 35mm macro for my Olympus E510 DSLR camera. As this camera uses the four-thirds system this 35mm lens is equivalent to a 70mm in the 35mm format.

Whether using a close up lens or a macro, when shooting from a close position to the subject you will need some form of steady support for your camera as even a small movement of the camera will render the spot you have focused on to be unsharp in the resulting image. I find a small tripod that I bought for table top photography to be sometimes more useful than my normal tripod. And, there are occasions when a beanbag is ideal. For instance, when I am lying down to capture a bloom that is at or just above ground level neither of my tripods will get low enough (I do have a Benbo tripod that would solve the problem but nowadays I find it too heavy to carry very far).

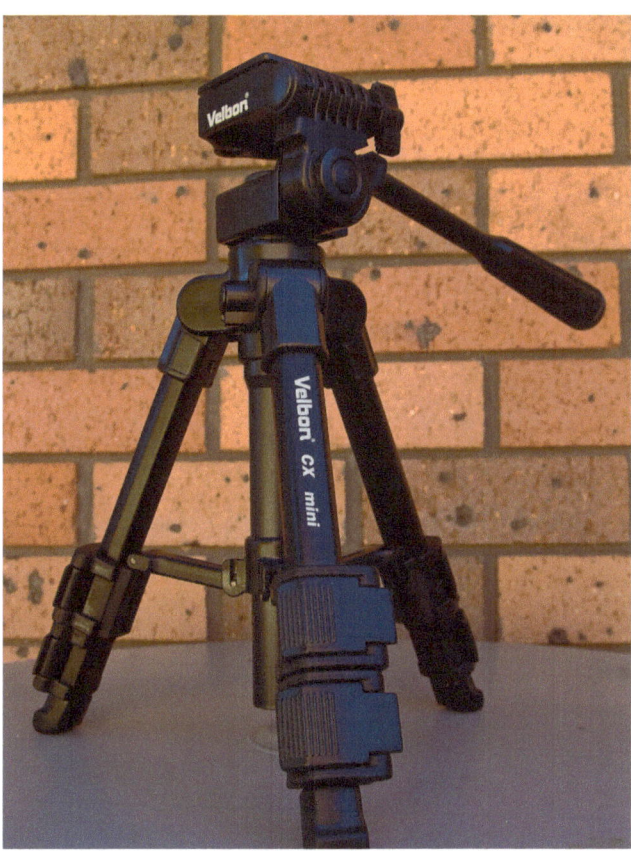

A mini tripod that I find useful for flower photography

Having said that, I have used my macro lens while hand holding my camera with some good and some dreadful results. It is just that sometimes opportunities have to be taken while they are there and setting up a tripod does take time. Nick Jenkins, a photographer from Wales, has produced some remarkable hand held shots with his macro lens. If there is a possibility of making a shot then I do recommend having a go.

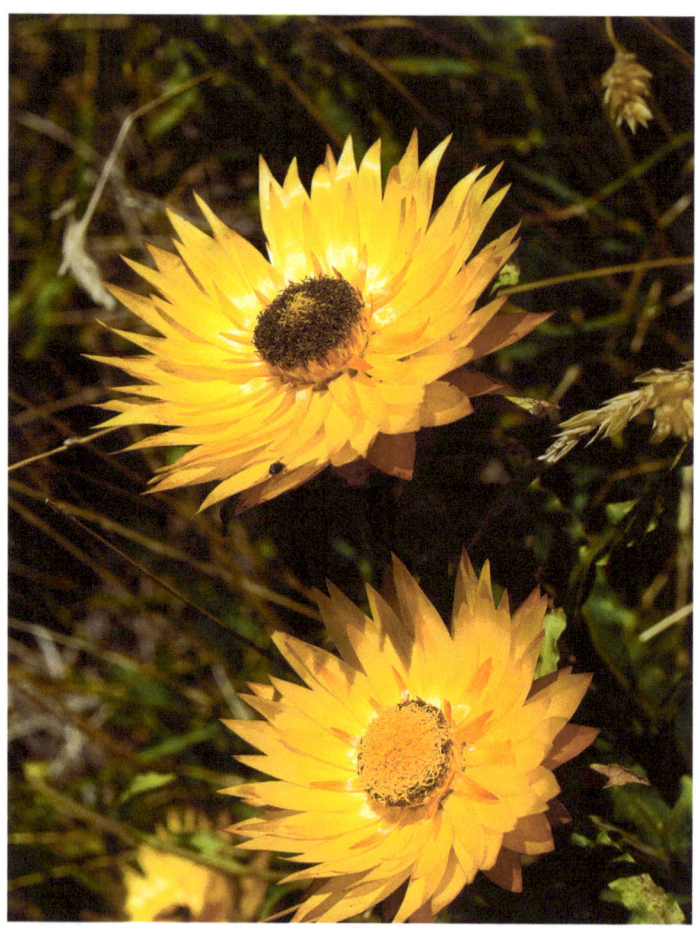

A hand held shot with a macro lens

I soon found that using a macro lens was a whole new ball game. My learning curve started with the focusing. Because of the shallow depth of field when focusing on a very close subject it is vital that you are able to choose what it is that you want to be sharp. I found that just relying on my auto focusing did not always achieve this. In fact, more often than not it failed. I tried using just manual focusing but with my lens I seemed to be turning the focusing ring forever so I then switched to Single Auto Focus plus Manual. This enabled me to roughly focus on the subject by depressing the shutter button halfway and then fine tuning to focus on the item that was important to me by using the manual focus. My flower shots began to look as I wanted them but I have a lot more to learn.

The shallow depth of field when using a large aperture generally works to our advantage in flower photography as anything outside the zone of focus is rendered as a totally abstract area of colour so concentrating the attention of the viewer on the subject. I often shoot at f5.6 or even wider but much depends on the size of the flower head as with a large bloom these wide apertures can put the edges of the flower out of focus. It is then that you have to use a smaller aperture to get all that you want in focus and it becomes important to watch the area behind the subject as it sometimes becomes distracting with semi-sharp items too noticeable. For a landscape photographer who is more often than not trying to get maximum depth of field this was an interesting change of thinking.

Macro lenses are not restricted to flower photography. Insects are ideal subjects although not that easy to capture. The best time to have a good chance of getting good results is in the early morning before their bodies have been warmed by the sun and they become active. Late afternoon can also be a possibility. When stalking insects do it slowly and try not to let a shadow from you or your camera fall over the subject otherwise they will not hang around to be captured. Once again, the aperture to choose depends on the size of the insect and the angle at which you are photographing it.

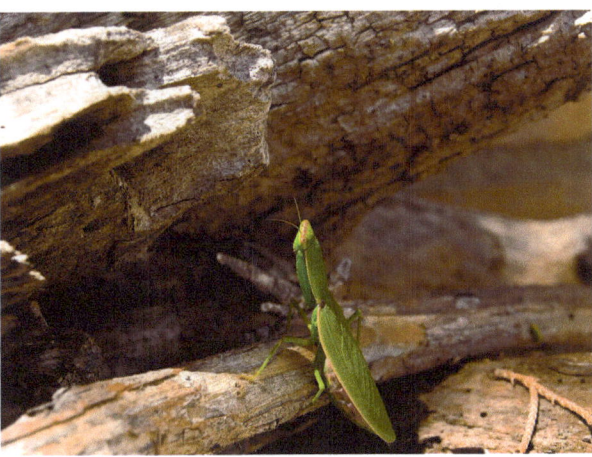

Macro lenses are made for insect photography. This was a shot that had to be made in a hurry so it was hand held. If I could have used a tripod, and if the insect would have waited, I would have shot much closer. As it is, if I want a larger image, I shall have to use my Perfect Resize software to enlarge it.

Having been a photographer a long time before digital, I have many files of transparencies in both 35mm and medium format sizes. While I have a good quality 35mm slide scanner I have only a flat bed for the medium format transparencies and negatives and that does not do justice to the originals. By using the macro lens to photograph these medium format images on my lightbox, I have found that I get some very worthwhile results. The camera is mounted on my table top tripod and I can use an aperture of f16 or f22 as the subject is flat. I have also found that some of my very old 35mm negatives that have experienced deterioration of the emulsion over time can be put on a lightbox and captured remarkably well by using my macro lens; the crazing of the emulsion is disguised by the lightbox which makes the cleaning of these images much less time consuming than when I use my film scanner which faithfully picks up all the problems.

There are many uses for a macro lens — or, for that matter, a set of close up lenses. As a writer, I sometimes need an image of something small to illustrate my words and the macro lens is ideal for filling that need.

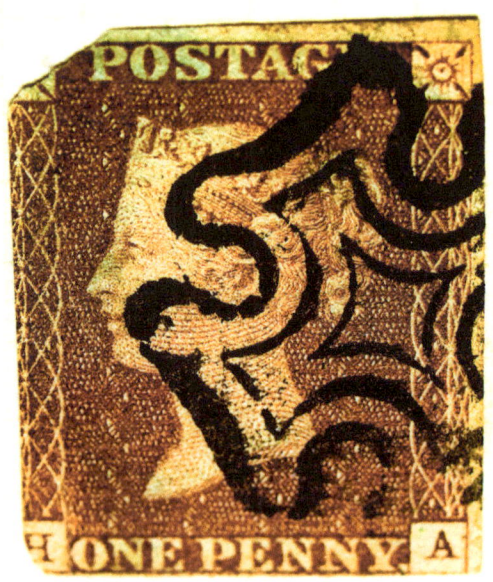

A macro lens shot of an early postage stamp

Of course, a macro lens is not restricted to just close up photography; it can be used for general shots in exactly the same way as any other lens.

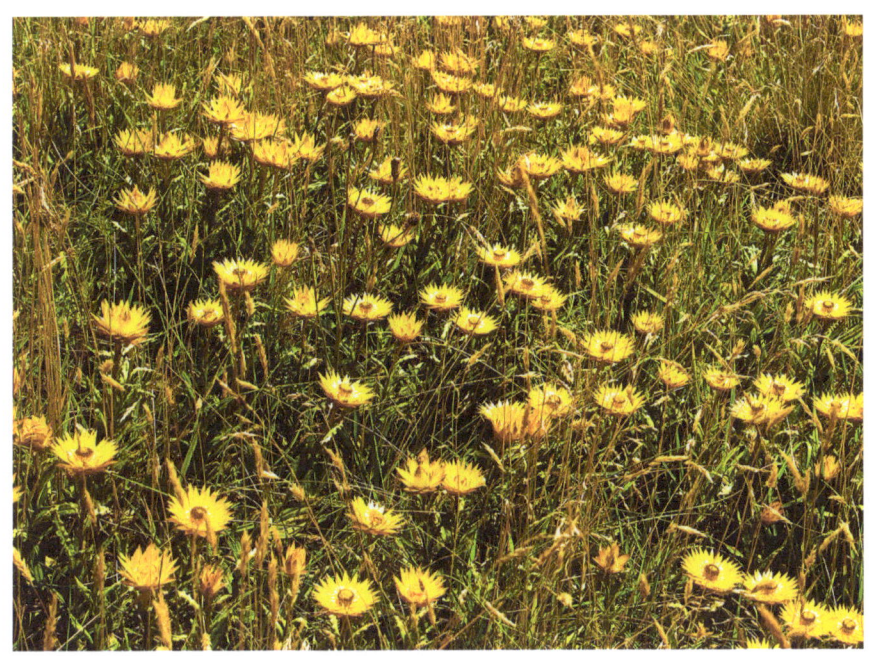

A macro lens used for a non close up shot.

I enjoy using my macro lens as it provides a definite change of approach from my landscape photography. I would like to develop further my capture of insects and especially butterflies but that will come with more practice.

If you want more information about the use of close up lenses I highly recommend Ross Hoddinott's book mentioned above and if you want a book on flower photography with special attention to macro lenses then I suggest that you have a look at *Bishop: Digital Flower Photography* (Photographers' Institute Press 978-1-86108-516-0).

The Micro Landscape

My introduction to the world of macro photography led me into a realisation that it is not always the big picture that I should be looking for when out to make my landscape images.

The flash of realisation hit me on a day when I 'needed' to make some pictures — as a photographer you will know what I mean — and the weather was against me. Uniformly grey cloud and lousy light are no recipe for great landscape shots.

With the itch in my shutter finger unsatisfied, I had to find a subject so I began casting around the area and, what do you know, there were dozens of them. Of course there were for those who have eyes to see. The big picture is made up of thousands, maybe millions of smaller pictures and this is what I had been missing. And for most of them I did not need my macro or close-up lenses.

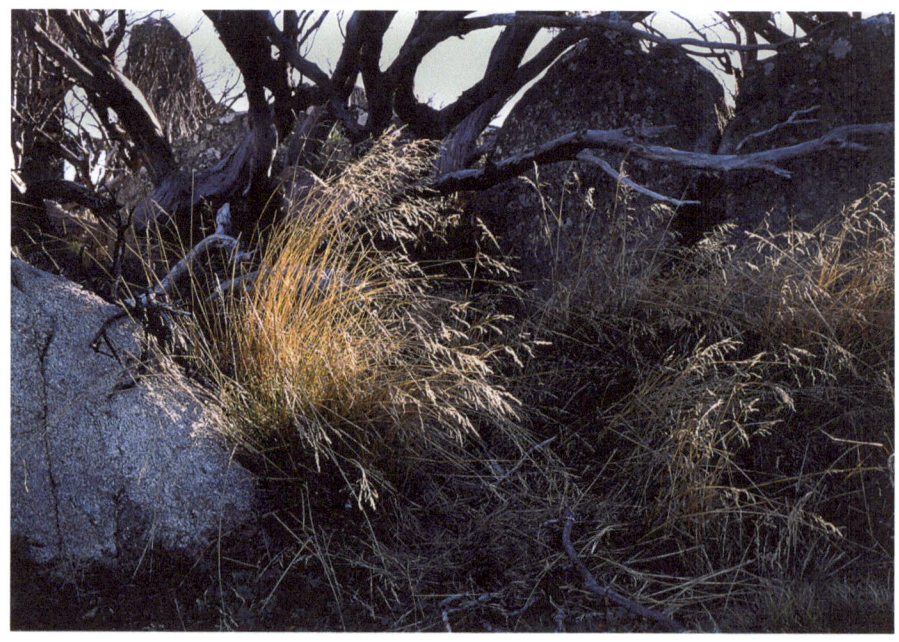

Sunlight just catching these dried grasses made the trek up the mountain worthwhile

It's not only the weather that can be against the making of the big picture. Sometimes it is hard to avoid the crowds in a popular spot for example but if we are attuned to looking within the scene for its components and are able to recognise potential pictures among them then our frustrations at not being able to take pictures because of situations that are beyond our control can be relieved.

And the same applies when the big picture just isn't right. Maybe it's the light that is wrong — from the wrong direction, at the wrong time of day — or something in the scene is just not photogenic and it can't be got around by moving it or moving our viewpoint. This happened to me recently when I went to the Snowy River in the New South Wales high country. The attractive scenes that I knew from a few years ago had disappeared in disastrous bushfires and the area had not fully recovered. There were dead trees everywhere and the whole area had a scrubby look about it. Its former beauty will come back but it will take a lot more time. So, in spite of the long drive to get there, any big picture scenes were out. I concentrated instead on close ups of some of the spring wildflowers that were brightening the river bank. It was the weather that first forced me into exploring for the smaller pictures but now it is my natural approach to landscape photography. I do not shun the big picture but now I am loath to leave a place until I have made some images that show something of its intimate details. I have learned to not only look but also to see.

And, that is the first step to making pictures of the micro-landscape, the bits that make up the whole. You may have heard the comment by camera club judges, "a well seen picture" and that is what we have to be aware of when considering our photography. We have to look and then, more importantly, we have to see the picture opportunities that present themselves. We have to take our time. We have to immerse ourselves in the area. We need to feel for the place. We need to experience wonder at the age of rock formations and how, over millennia, they have been fashioned by wind and water, at the way in which trees and other plants survive in less than perfect conditions, how they cling to life and overcome obstacles by growing round and over them. We need to be in awe of the power of nature.

I try not to have pre-conceived ideas of what I am looking for as subjects when I begin to explore. To do so would defeat the object of the exercise which is to first look and then to see. However, depending on the location, there are some obvious subjects that crop up repeatedly. For instance, in the Snowy Mountains the twisted and contorted trunks of snow gums, the bases of the same trees which often incorporate huge boulders, the wildflowers that fill the alpine meadows in high summer, the fallen golden leaves of the deciduous trees in autumn and, in the winter, the plants that brave the snow, the creeks winding between snowy banks and the footprints of animals and birds in otherwise undisturbed snow.

On the coast, there are the rock pools, gouged out by centuries of water action, and their inhabitants, rippled sand, flotsam and jetsam, the plants that bind the sand, and the many wonderful shapes of rock platforms.

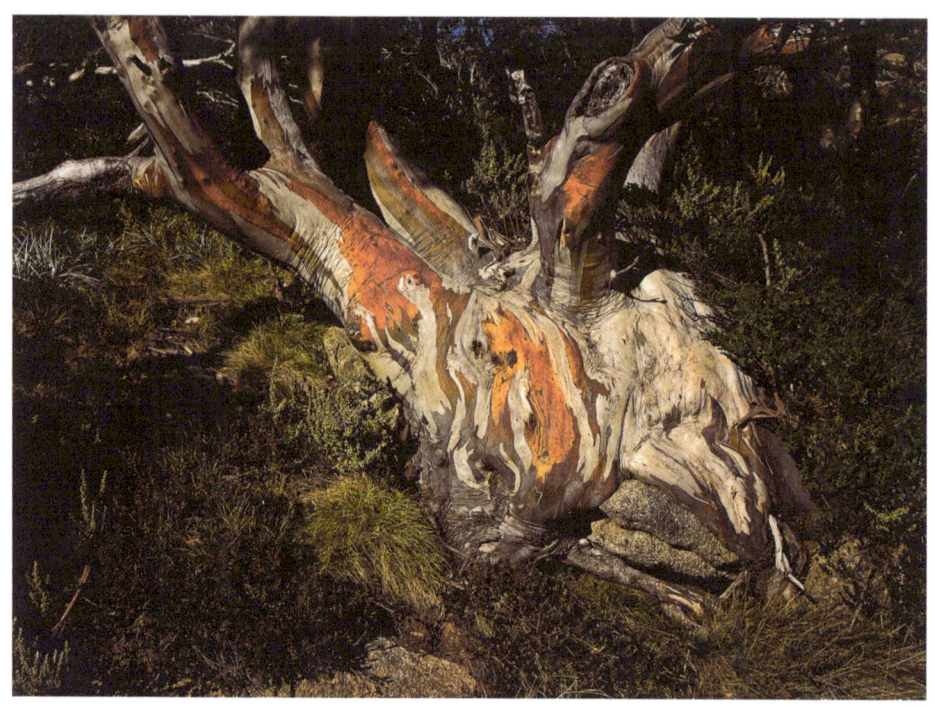

A tortured and twisted snow gum high in the Snowy Mountains in Australia. Note the granite boulders over which the tree's trunk has grown.

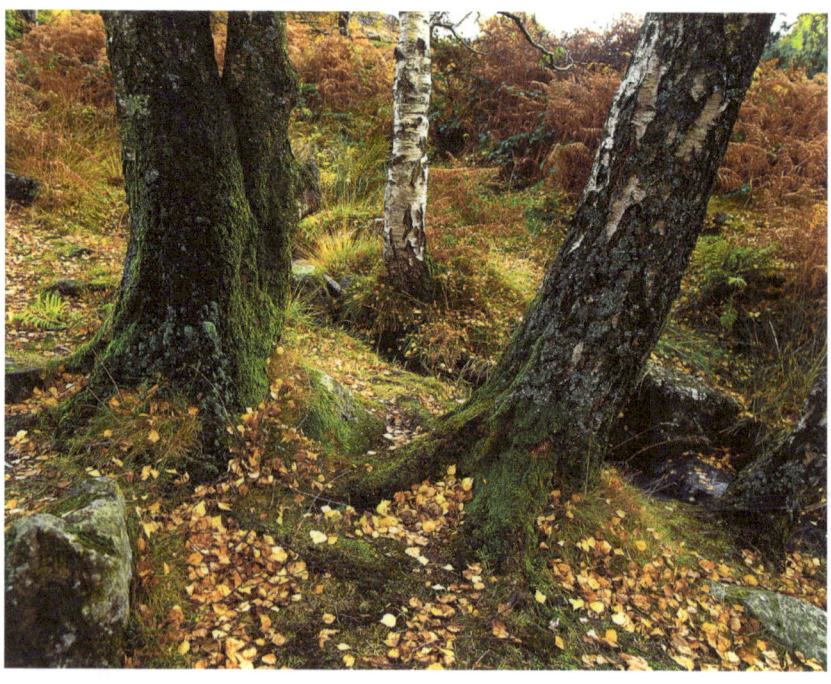

Autumn leaves under an overcast sky in the English Lake District

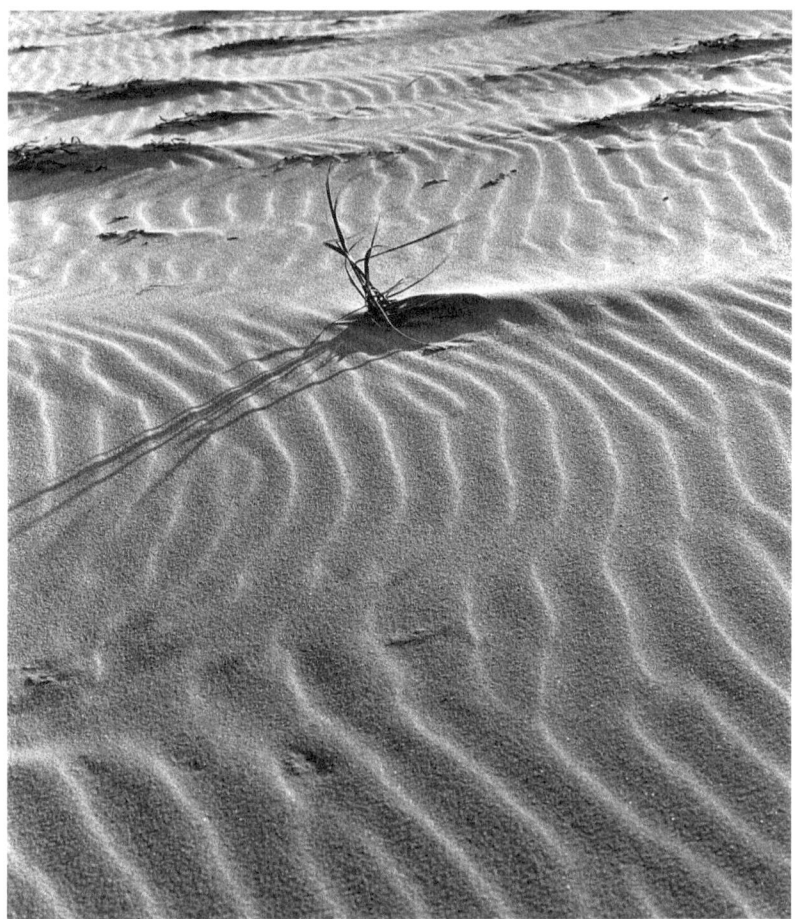

A black and white shot that works well because of the patterns formed by the rippled sand and the shadows thrown by the plant that has pushed through the sand.

Wherever you are, look up. Sometimes a wonderful, and generally fleeting, cloud arrangement will make a great image. And there may be a photogenic arrangement of leaves on a tree or at your feet. Check the trunks of trees, especially after or even during rain when the bark of some gum trees is magnificently coloured. Watch the swirling water in creeks — apart from anything else flowing water is very therapeutic and calming — especially where it ripples over boulders.

Then there are the grasses, especially when backlit or windblown, or flowers or fungi, or fallen trees or . . . the list is infinite.

Those are just some examples but it doesn't matter where you go or where you live, you will find subjects to fill your viewfinder if you really look.

Close-up images of flowers are often better when made under overcast skies as the reduction in contrast suits the subject and enhances the colours. I carry a plastic sheet when expecting to do close-up work at ground level to make the job a little more comfortable especially in muddy conditions.

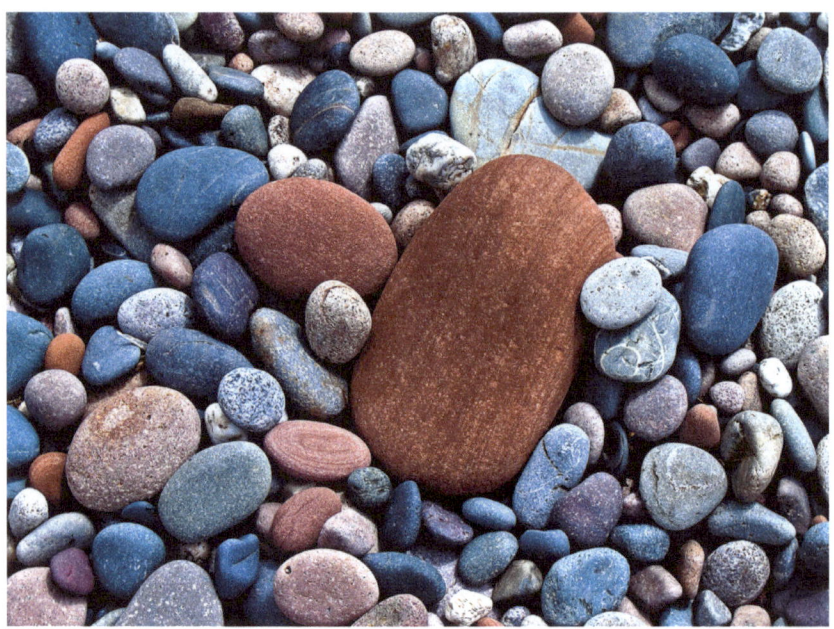

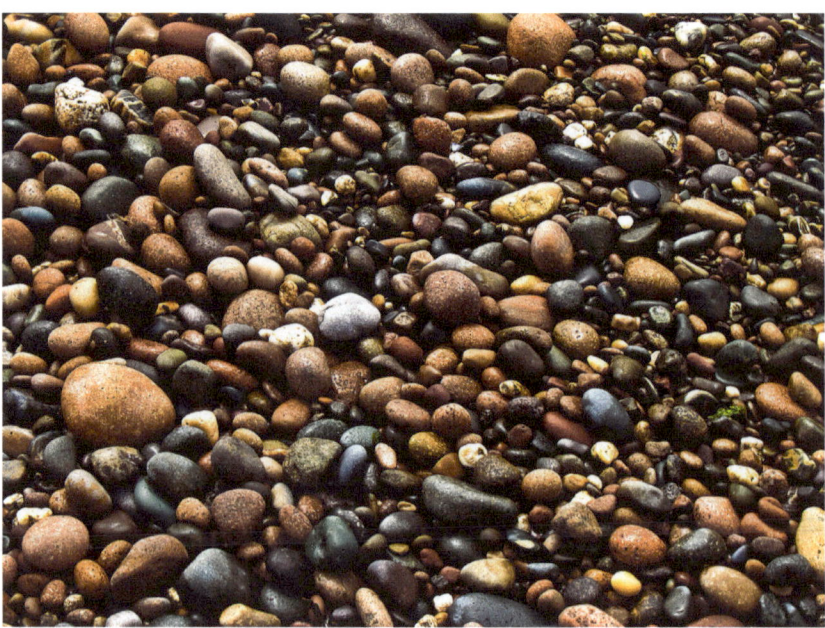

Two coastal shots. How much better the first would have been if the stones were wet as in the lower image. It's worth carrying a container to get some water in when photographing on a beach.

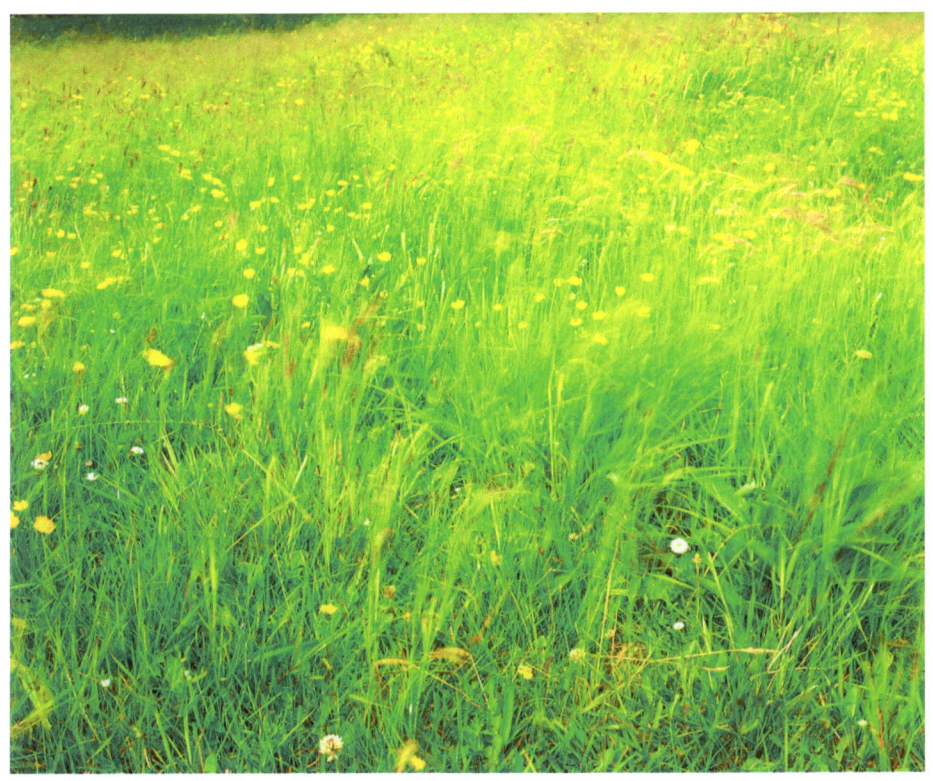

Windblown grass and wildflowers in the English Lake District on a dull day.

When the light level is a little low, you may want to use some fill-in flash to enhance your subject. Most DSLRs will allow you to adjust the flash setting — my Olympus lets me adjust the flash output in one third stop increments. I have found that reducing the output by one or two thirds works well most of the time. In pre-digital days before the very useful histogram, I produced good results with a very basic flash gun by shooting through one or two layers of a white handkerchief. Not very scientific but it did work. But, do experiment with your equipment before you leave home!

Aluminium foil can also be useful to bounce light into your subject and it is worth carrying some in your camera bag. I have a Space Blanket which I bought many years ago which is very useful as a reflector. I can also wrap myself in it if I get lost and have to spend the night outdoors in low temperatures!

One question that crops up every now and then about the photographing of the natural world is: do we take the picture exactly as it is found or can we move things around and even import an item from somewhere else? As far as I'm concerned, that is up to you! For the record, I do clear away distracting items, some grass for instance, and I have been known to introduce a greenish leaf from a few centimetres away on to a pile of autumn coloured leaves to provide some contrast. But, if I can, I leave it as I found it. If I do make changes they are only minor. But, it's your picture and your choice. Whether you use digital or film, or colour or black and white, is immaterial. It is the result that counts and that result will come from your ability to see the picture in the first place and then from your technical know-how which will enable you to make the image.

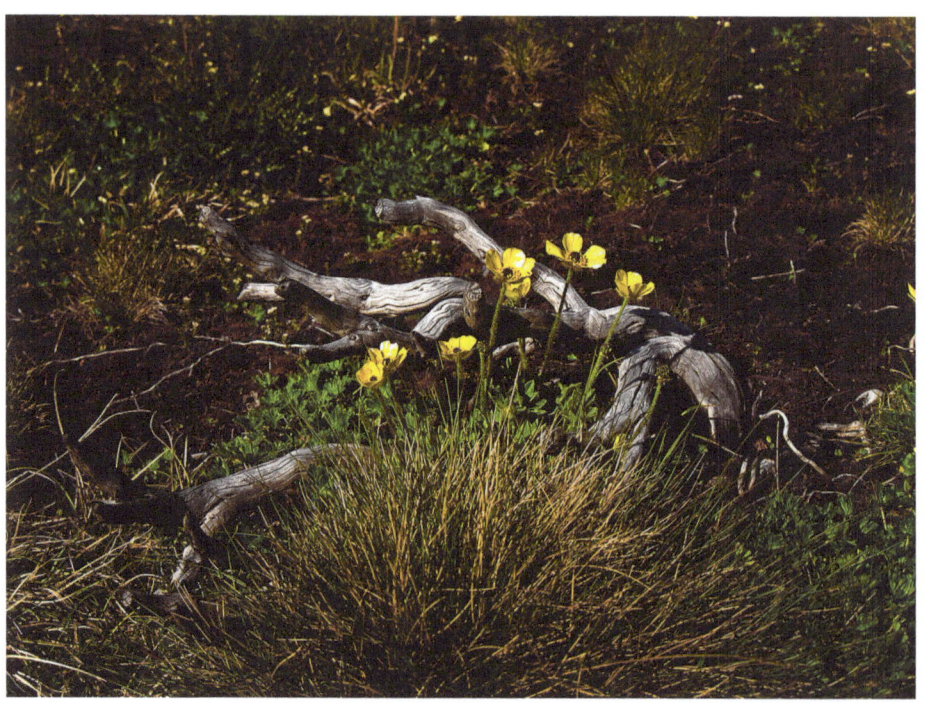

Shot under a semi-overcast sky.

Contact

If you have any questions, e-mail me at
dbigwoodphotography@bigpond.com
and I shall try to answer them.

To see my Facebook photography page, go to
http://tinyurl.com/n9sd3cx

My blog and website page is at
http://davidbigwoodpublishing. wordpress.com

Some of my prints are for sale at
http://davidbigwood.zenfolio.com

To see my photographs at Alamy, the on-line photo library, see
http://tinyurl.com/p4xzzrs

Other photography e-books in Kindle format by David Bigwood available at your Amazon store

Starting Freelance Photography — *The basic steps needed to start freelance photography.*

Images that SELL — *Over 30 images that have been published. A useful handbook for freelance photographers.* **Also available as a print on demand paperback.**

Starting Nature Photography — *Introduction to nature photography including wildflowers, birds on the wing, snow, with photos of animals, insects, flowers, and demonstration of processing with Photoshop.*

Introduction to Filters for Digital Photography — *An introduction to the important filters for use in digital photography especially of the landscape and a process to obtain fine images from a contrasty original.*

Black and White Photography in the Digital Age — *How to convert colour images to black and white using Photoshop, how to use Photoshop's duotone, processing a black and white image, simulate processes such as split toning, sepia toning, lith printing, selenium toning and cross processing.* **Also available as a print on demand paperback.**

Into the Light - an introduction to backlit or contre jour photography — *How to rid yourself of the 'sun over your shoulder' mantra and add the wow factor to your pictures by shooting into the light. How to calculate exposure, look for subjects, avoid flare, make silhouettes and make your people subjects comfortable. Many examples of images included.*

Optimize Your Portraits - how to get the best results consistent with reality — *How to process your portrait shots to get the best results without losing the reality of the subject. In other words, how to make the final print as faithful to the subject as possible and not over process so that your sixty year old sitter has the skin of a sixteen year old. Also how to concentrate the viewer's attention on the subject.*

How to Show Movement in Your Still Photography — *Shows the ways in which movement can be shown in a still photograph. Demonstrates the use of blur, panning, freezing and also how Photoshop can be used. Additional information on the* *making of abstract images by moving the camera while exposing and post-processing with Photoshop to produce abstract pictures.*

Images of the High Country of New South Wales — *An e-book of over 50 photographs from the photogenic area of the Snowy Mountains of Australia from David Bigwood, a Licentiate of the Royal Photographic Society.*

Cash from Your Camera — *How to make souvenirs using your pictures — How to make bookmarks, greeting cards, calendars, notecards, postcards, posters using your photos. Illustrated to show how products are set out for printing at home as well as advice on using a commercial printer. Written by a self publisher of souvenirs to be sold through retailers.*

How to Photograph Birds on the Wing — *Details the author's learning curve in seeking to photograph birds in flight. Illustrated with pictures that complement the text. The details in this Kindle book are in the author's e-book, Starting Nature Photography so if you have that book, do not buy this one.*

How to do Well in Photography Competitions — *What to look for when entering photography competitions. The benefits for your photography and how to get the 'wow' factor. Illustrated with example pictures and step by step instruction for processing images.*

How to Improve Your Digital Photography — *An e-book based on my topic e-books including Introduction to Filters for Digital Photography, Black and White Photography in the Digital Age, Optimize Your Portraits, How to do Well in Competitions, Into the Light, How to Show Movement in Still Photography, Starting Macro Photography, Starting Nature Photography. It is aimed at beginners to intermediate photographer to help them improve their photography.* **Also available in two volumes.**

The Black and White Enthusiast: How the author processes his black and white images — *I am a black and white enthusiast and this book is intended to show the beauty of black and white photography and how I go about achieving my results. I hope it may turn you from somebody interested in the black and white genre to a real Black and White Enthusiast.*

Make Your Photography Pay — *This e-book is a compilation of some of my e-books on individual topics including Starting Freelance Photography, Images that Sell, How to Make Souvenirs Using Your Pictures, and Put Words with Your Pictures.* **Also available as a print on demand paperback.**

Photographers' Introduction to the Boudoir — *This book talks about finding models/clients, what to do when you have found one, posing, selling the results, shooting in colour or black and white and finishes with a gallery of ideas*